*S*i

MW01596885

BUSINESS OPTIMIZATION STRATEGY SERIES

Lead Generation
Development

**Stephen Pierce's Business Optimization Strategy Series –
Lead Generation Development**

Stephen Pierce International, Inc.
101 Washington, # 214
Whitney, Texas 76692
(866) 272-1410

TABLE OF CONTENTS:

Chapter 1: Aggressive Tactics

Every business needs a solid lead generation system in place. In order to get those leads, you have to get aggressive in your tactics. You are ready to design particular processes to make this happen.

The Draw

When you understand your market segments, you know how, when, and why your customers buy from you. You also know who they are and what influences them to make the purchase. Once you have that information, you're ready to put it into a lead generation model. This model will help you to capture leads which will convert into new customers.

Regardless of what you are selling, you have to have a draw on the front end. This attractive draw pulls customers in to your business. Once you've got them hooked, you're in a good position to make the sale.

Retail stores use coupons, publications or informational marketers to draw people into their facilities. Websites use landing pages, banner ads or pop-up ads to proposition web users again and again. If you only have one shot to make the sale, your chances

are slim. If you have repeated shots, your odds improve greatly.

When people hit a web page and then decide to leave, they are done. They aren't coming back. You want to have something that compels them to stay on the site and then opt-in.

Aggressive Approach to Capturing Leads

You must have an aggressive approach to capturing leads. With a particular client, we designed a marketing and selling system for the company. On the front end, we designed two lead generation pages—a short version and a long version.

If a prospect doesn't opt in from the short version, he is then presented with the long version of that page. If he doesn't opt-in from the long version, then the product they were looking to sell comes up on the page. If does not buy the product, he is given 11 reasons why he should own the product and a special bonus offer.

If he exits, another pop-up page appears that highlights the frequently asked questions about the product as well as a second bonus offer. If he doesn't act on that offer, another page pops up, asking a question. After that point, he is given a third bonus offer. If he still doesn't make the purchase, we start to reduce the price on the product.

This process involves dealing with different objections. We don't know why a person is leaving the page. We first present the prospect with the lowest decision barriers. We are not asking them for a credit card or any other piece of personal information. The only information requested is their name and email address.

If the person landed on the page, we can assume they have some kind of interest in the product. At this point, we don't want to let them off the hook. These people aren't bookmarking your landing page. They are on and then quickly off the page. As a result, you have to hook them.

Since the issue is keeping them on the page, you have to get aggressive when they try to exit. I have done some crazy things to get leads. Some things I did out of stupidity. Others I did as pure experimentation to see what would actually work.

On one site, I had a pop-up that would take over the entire screen. If someone decided to leave the page, this pop-up would cover everything, including your computer's start menu. You couldn't see anything but this entire graphic covering your screen. There were only two ways to get past this pop-up. You either had to click on the graphic, which was what I wanted, or you had to reboot your entire computer.

It seems like an unappealing tactic but I was getting some serious clicks. I'm sure I was upsetting a lot of people, but at the same time, I was also converting leads.

Think Outside the Box

When you think of aggressive marketing, imagine you are having a conversation with somebody. You need to tell this person something incredibly important. It is life-saving. You need the person to listen but she is distracted and trying to leave the room. You then block her exit, telling her to stay. She has to stay so you can finish what you have to say. It's just like that.

I did end up taking that extreme pop-up ad down but it's a good example of an aggressive tactic. I had another intense tactic. When people would try to leave the site, I had a script on the page that would open their email client. A new email would be created with it pre-addressed to me with a pre-filled subject line and email body.

All they had to do was click "send." I received some negative feedback on those emails. I didn't end up keeping either of those particular aggressive techniques but they were part of my experimentation process. It's all about thinking outside the box.

Sometimes you have to experiment with a variety of different tactics before you find the ones that work well for your business. You cannot be scared to try. Don't let fear keep you stagnant.

Finding Balance

If you have something of great value, you must find the balance between aggressive pushing and respect. If somebody leaves your website, you attempt to capture the lead by giving them a higher proposition of value.

If you were a face-to-face salesperson, you wouldn't let someone walk out the door the first moment they said no. You would repeatedly try to win them over. The same goes for the online world. You can't let the first negative response get you down. If you're hungry, you can't listen to objections.

It isn't surprising that the majority of people that come to any site are going to exit. Whether you're selling something directly or you have a multiple step opt-in process, most people are going to choose to leave the site, regardless of the level of value. That's just the way things work.

As a result, you must realize it's about more than the content itself. You can have stellar content and still have people leaving. The sequential activities make the sale. The gentle pressure you apply pulls people into your lead generation pool.

If you're adding real value to your marketplace, you have to fight for your leads a bit. Don't make it easy for them to walk away from you. Get aggressive.

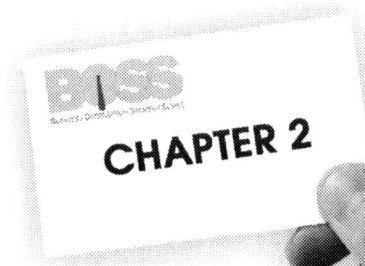

Chapter 2: Take Every Opportunity

Every visitor to your website is an opportunity. If the person tries to leave, you may have to give them an additional bonus to get them to stay. It is worth it though because every visitor is an opportunity. Every person is an opportunity to cultivate a relationship.

Track Your Opportunities

We have a product, Fibonacci Secrets, that has done over a million dollars in sales. We were able to track leads incredibly effectively. Even when affiliates send us people, we had a sub-tracking system in place.

We would then track each visitor's behavior. Whether they came via affiliates or one of our mailings, we could track their behavior. We would then see whether they made the purchase immediately or after opting into our sequential process. Over $114,000 came directly from the opt-in sequence. That sequence had incredible value. If we did not have that sequence in place, over $100,000 in sales would have been completely missed.

That's about 10% of the total sales volume. You can't afford to lose that kind of money. You must have a good sequence in place that serves as a solid way to capture those leads.

Another method we used involved placing a different tracking link in each follow-up email. After the lead was captured, the follow-up email gave them detailed information as well as a unique bonus. It also restated the guarantee in a different manner.

In that sequence, most of the clicks took place in the fifth email. Again, we see how important the sequence is. These unique tracking links can be easily used in any auto-responder system.

Lead Generation Model Finding

There are six steps in the lead generation model finding system.

1. Find your area of specialization.

Consider the market you're in, the problem you're looking to solve and your priorities in addressing that issue. Think very specifically. As you consider your specialty, you have to relate it to your driving force. If you're user-driven, you need to address all your customers' needs in relation to your particular market. This line of thinking will help you find your specialty.

For example, a particular business is driven by women over 40 years old. We put together a variety of different ideas around that target market. We discovered her driving force and a specific plan to properly address their target market.

If the company wanted to target menopausal women specifically, the strategy would be totally different. It wasn't that narrow a group though. It was all women over 40.

Your area of specialization falls in line with all the other things we've covered. Your driving force, areas of excellence and target market all fit into where your specialization will lie. By now, you're likely beginning to see how everything ties together. Each part of the process is a strong and powerful link in the complete chain of progress.

2. Develop lead generation content.

You need content. This can be simple reports or data. For instance, consider a report on the subject of losing weight without dieting. People who hate dieting would undoubtedly want to download that report.

Even if someone is skeptical, you're not asking them for much. You aren't asking for money. You're only trying to generate a lead. With a catchy content headline, you can draw people in.

3. Package the content.

You need the content in a useful, attractive format. This could be in a PDF or mp3. It involves formatting the content in a solid manner. For example, you could outline seven ways to lose weight without dieting.

You now have two titles, "How to Lose Weight Without Dieting" and "Seven Things You Must Do to Lose Weight Without Dieting." On the landing page, you could put the first headline. Underneath that headline, list the benefits of the report. Then have a clear link to the actual report titled, "Seven Things You Must Do to Lose Weight Without Dieting." You now have a clear connection between both titles.

4. Attract the target market.

There are various ways to attract traffic. From Smart Opt-in Pages and affiliates to blogs and RSS articles, you can use a variety of different means to draw in new traffic.

Use ways that you know work quickly and effectively to generate both short-term and long-term traffic. You have to consider ways to generate traffic immediately as well as ways to develop stability in long-term growth.

5. Compel the target market.

Attracting the target market is different than compelling the target market. You've tracked the target market as they came to your site. At this point, something else needs to happen. You have to compel them to take action.

You've already attracted them. You've done what was necessary to get them to your site. The compelling part begins when the conversions start to take place. You first have to get them to the place where they want to get that additional information.

6. Convert the traffic into leads.

In this phase, you need to suggest and find. First, you have to be clear on your specialty area. If you know your specialization, you'll be in touch with your target market. You'll know what they need and want, and develop your content around those things.

You convert leads by working with the client. You suggest and find solutions for them based on the conversation you have.

Create a Cheat Sheet

Write your specialty on a piece of paper. Now, write out your specific target market. List the problems you are trying to solve as well as the information your target market is seeking.

This paper can serve as a cheat sheet for you. You can use this information as you create your content. Go to www.BOSSMembership.com to download your Cheat Sheet.

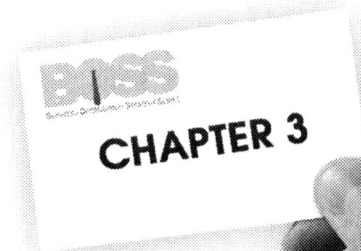

Chapter 3: Content Specifics

As you create your content, you need to ensure it is absolutely high-quality. The creation process should be detailed and specific, to ensure you are providing high value to both leads and customers.

Problem-solving Tactics

You must be good at solving problems if you wish to have continued success. When you have a problem, you must first define what the issue is. Next, determine why the problem is occurring. Only after you've defined the problem and why it occurs can you begin to solve it.

We've discussed the issue of the leaky faucet, the wet floor underneath the sink is the problem. You can put a bucket underneath the faucet to catch the water. This prevents the floor from getting wet but it's just a temporary fix.

This fix does not address the question of, "Why does this problem occur?" If you answer that question, you'll determine that it's a broken pipe. You can, at that point, replace the pipe and fix the issue.

11

When you solve a problem, you must look at the root cause of the issue. You can then also put preventative measures in place. As you give your target marketplace content, consider giving them preventative measures to address their problems.

The same goes for opportunities. Show people how to make opportunities happen. You can leverage and then exploit an opportunity once it occurs.

Problem solving and opportunity exploitation are two great frameworks that you can use in your content. They will certainly help you generate leads.

Information Teaser

Create a one-page informational teaser. This is one page of content that leaves people wanting more. If you have enough powerful content on one page, you can deliver that content effectively to gain leads.

You can then later develop a detailed information pack. This pack can have multiple elements, including checklists, surveys and questionnaires.

Free checklists are great tools to draw people into your business. Think of them as link bait. They will help you generate traffic.

The same goes for questionnaires. Some of the best questionnaires are those that give the user information. The users can fill out the answers and tally their scores. They are then given some sort of revelation about themselves as a result of their scores.

When you create these questionnaires, you should attempt to slant them in your favor. For example, you could have a questionnaire with a total possible score of 100. If the participant scores less than 80, he is in need of your service. If he scores 80 to 100, he could use your service but it isn't critical. If he scores less than 60, he better get your service immediately. This is how you use questionnaires to generate business.

Proper Packaging

Your content packaging will be influenced by your strategy. Ideally, you want to have more than just a name and email address. If you're hoping to send them more powerful content, it's useful to have a fax number, phone number and mailing address.

People are more willing to give out their email addresses than their physical mailing addresses and phone numbers. If you have a really powerful PDF file, you can use that via email marketing but for physical content packages, you need mailing addresses.

If you want the more detailed information, you should offer something physical. People will have no issue giving their mailing address if you are offering them something physical.

Lead Generation Programs

We designed a lead generation program for a client and implemented it in just two and a half days. We put up the website, featuring a video we wrote, taped and produced. We synced up music and audio in a very short period of time. We had the whole site ready extremely fast.

We generated over 5,700 leads. These leads included names, physical addresses and phone numbers. That lead generation campaign was incredibly successful.

Many people desire a custom lead generation program. While a lead generation process is powerful, you must have a solid selling

process in place. Otherwise, you'll just have a lot of leads without much revenue.

You can get excited about your leads and be distracted from the fact that you're not actually selling. It's easy to over-invest in getting leads and under-invest in the selling process. Avoid this by setting the foundation of a solid selling system beforehand.

Retool Your Packaging

There are a variety of different methods for packaging content. You can have mp3s, PDFs, CDs, DVDs and videos. In addition, there are e-books, membership sites, webinars and tutorials.

With our Optimization Series website, we offered a two-hour video of Jay Abraham for free. It was the first time there was ever a free video of Jay Abraham available. We had it online after our Unleash Your Marketing Genius event.

In order to view the video, you had to log into the site. You didn't have to pay anything to view it but you did have to log in. If you weren't already a member of the site, you had to create a user ID and password.

We know our strategy. We continue to put up more quality content. We are setting it up as a premium content site. We will then introduce one-year all-access passes to all the premium content.

We're giving them great content for free. We're just going to keep it going. We're building a base of users who like to read the blog and articles. They like to listen to the audios and podcasts, and watch the videos.

It's multi-dimensional, meaning we're giving them content in different formats. By doing so, we match different modalities.

We're confident that when we introduce them to that premium content, it will go well.

In the process, we're taking our time. We understand what we're doing. While we're generating leads, we understand our long-term selling process.

You can't get stuck in the short-term. You have to hold onto your long-term vision. Some people may think we should have charged to view the video. The long-term value of all those new accounts to our website outweighed the possible benefit of charging to view the video. It's all about long-term vision.

Chapter 4: Your Target Market

You are targeting your product or service to a particular segment of the marketplace. You must tap into that target market in order to achieve success. When you do so, you'll notice better conversions and higher revenue.

Smart Opt-in Page sites work extremely well. Affiliates, blogs, RSS feeds and articles also help to tap into that target market. In addition, press releases help to generate leads by getting the word out about your business.

Before you start to generate that traffic, you must have everything in place. This means your landing page and selling process are established and ready to go.

White papers are another tool you can use. A white paper is essentially content. It can be in the form of a PDF. Because it's been labeled a white paper, there is a distinct level of value placed on it.

Corporations have white papers that are based on detailed research. Generally, this research is conducted in various markets and on particular case studies. The results are then analyzed and decisions are made based on those conclusions.

Consider Your Topic

When it comes to aggressively going after your target market, it's important to consider your topic. For example, if you are in the business of self improvement, you have to be aware of the language you use in the sales process. Instead of a hard sell, ask leads what their current line of thinking is going to cost them in the next 24 hours.

You can even start by asking what it will cost them in the next week or even the next year. You just need to put a finite timeline on it. By doing so, you create a sense of urgency. You are trying to prevent a catastrophe from happening in their lives.

Habitual ways of thinking can create catastrophes. You need your prospective customers to see that. They need to see what could happen in a worst case scenario. They can then opt-in and choose to avoid that possibility.

Give Them Multiple Chances

Exit pop-ups are still effective today. If you are tracking your numbers, you'll see a boost on your opt-ins if you add exit pop-up ads. They may not be as effective as they used to be, but you will still notice improvements when you use them. Try adding a few and see the effect it has on your numbers.

You have to think about reasons why they may be bailing out without opting-in first. Hit them multiple times, giving them a lot of chances to take action. Put some heat on them.

Experimentation is key. Put up a ridiculous offer for a day and see what effects that has. Try making your content more detailed, or your packaging more attractive.

Add variety to your packaging. Rather than just a simple PDF, offer prospects a PDF with an audio file and then a separate questionnaire. Make it a detailed informational package which leads can download.

Give the option of a physical version of the packet. You can even charge shipping and handling. If people are getting something physical, they are often willing to pay some small cost. Just make sure that the content you send is valuable. You'll also find that people will pay for a physical version, even if they can get an online version for free. It feels more valuable to them if they can hold it in their hands.

It's then your responsibility to follow-up with these people. If you don't, you may never hear from them again. You've given them this valuable information for free. It's your responsibility to repeatedly follow up to make sure those relationships become valuable to you.

Fight for Your Leads

Marketing is a game of missing information. You have to make them want that missing information. You have to find the balance between being aggressive and respectful. You can maintain this balance by being honest with the prospect. Be aggressive but tell them why you are being aggressive.

People are often turned off by aggression. You don't want them to opt-out so explain the issue early on in the process. Address it up front. Don't just let them see the opt-out link and leave. Tell them early on, "You can leave but it will be a huge mistake."

You are essentially telling them that you are fighting for them. Let them know that you are concerned for their future. You understand their need and you are there to fulfill it. If they opt-out and leave you, they are shutting down one of their biggest supporters.

19

Use the right language and they will understand. You can even say, "I'm being persistent because I care," or "I want to help you; that's why I keep trying." This language will curb a lot of people from dropping out of the process. It will boost your sales and some people will actually start to respond to you. They will understand your aggressive tactics.

Chapter 5: The Importance of the Follow-up

The follow-up is an essential part of your selling process. If you don't follow up with prospects, you'll lose out on an astounding number of conversions. You can easily follow-up with people via an auto-responder sequence. The sequence will continuously drip information to them.

Passive and Active Information

You can set your auto-responder to send both passive and dynamic information. It is passive because you pre-load the auto-responder with this fixed information. It doesn't change.

You can also set up dynamic updates. If you notice something relevant on Google News or another news source, you can go in and manually send out an email based on that recent information. With the dynamic updates, you custom-make exactly what the emails say.

You are then giving the prospects two different dimensions. You are providing the passive information but also giving them up-to-date dynamic data. You then keep people hooked in because they love these cutting-edge updates. They will begin to consider you a premium source for that information.

Remember, reliability precedes profitability. Once you establish yourself as a reliable and dependable source for content and news, you become a reliable and dependable source from which to purchase.

It's ideal because you become their information source. They don't feel they have to go search for this information because you provide it. If it's relevant, they know it's going to come over from you.

For example, with our Fibonacci Series, we would throw in some fun facts from time-to-time. People were expecting to get email information about Fibonacci trading. We would also include Fibonacci facts, such as ratios. The Fibonacci ratio of the arm to the body is 1.6. Little facts like this keep people interested. It adds some additional flavor to your emails so people can actually enjoy them more.

We would also include dynamic updates. For example, we may say that wheat was just in over a trace, and it bounced off the fifty percent Fibonacci retracement level with a bullish reverse. That would be a dynamic update since it is timely and relevant. It's news-worthy.

We would then mix in some passive information. Details on the history of Fibonacci would be passive since that information is not going to change. It's all about creating that balance between dynamic and passive information.

Remember, people are hungry for information. Whether they use the information or not, they still like to have it. It's a bit like rubber-necking. It's people showing that they are nosy. They want to know what is going on.

You've got a hook because they are nosy. Then you provide powerful content. Your content is so compelling and engaging, they aren't able to walk away from you. At that point, they move from being a potential customer to being an actual customer.

The Power of the Physical

Try sending people physical versions of your product. You'll likely see your numbers increase. Do some split-testing. Offer only electronic versions such as downloadable materials for a while. Then offer physical versions that you actually ship to them. See which packaging gives you better results. Make sure to track the results with each version.

You can always keep both in place but you have to know which works better for you. Oftentimes, the two can work in concert with each other. A prospective client might download a bit of information via a link. He may then request additional information via a mailing. You tease him with a little electronic information then you convert him via a robust physical informational packet. Make your two versions work together.

You could also offer a physical version, and if he doesn't take that, you could offer a downloadable version for a cheaper price. Again, the content has to be high-quality. You don't want the person to feel like he didn't get good value for his dollar.

For example, a person sees the physical version and decides not to buy it. Perhaps she doesn't want to pay for shipping or maybe the total product price is too expensive. She tries to exit. Then she gets an option to buy the downloadable version so there's no shipping involved.

In addition to the lack of shipping costs, you also offer the product at a cheaper price. You can justify the lower price because an electronic product is almost always going to be cheaper than a physical product. At this point, she decides to buy.

You can then also sell her a back-up version. This is still less than the entire physical version. You still make money on the deal, you converted a lead and the customer is happy.

You sell the back-up copy as coverage in case of emergencies. People never know what is going to happen to their computers so it's always a good idea to have a back-up CD.

You can even set a price for the physical or back-up versions that includes shipping. You can then tell customers that you are covering the shipping costs. They only have to pay for the CD cost. Just make sure you set prices so you always make a profit.

While you certainly want to convert as many leads as possible, make sure to assess the financial outcome of each sale. You should be making a profit on each and every action. In the beginning, it may be a very slim profit because you are looking at the long-term value of individual client relationships. Just make sure you are considering revenue at every step of the process.

Chapter 6: Act on Your Knowledge

This entire process is all about you. It's about optimizing your business and helping you get the results that you want. At this point in the process, things start to fit together.

Initially, your vision, mission statement and driving force might seem separate. You may have even wondered why they matter. Now, they all start to fit together cohesively. You can begin to execute a lot of the process. Once you do so, you'll start to see results.

As you progress, you'll be ready to think more deeply about pricing. It involves the sweet spot of not overpricing or under-pricing your product or service. If you overprice, people will walk away without making the purchase. If you under-price, you leave too much on the table and it negatively affects your overall profitability.

You can ultimately let the market determine your pricing structure. Based on that market price, you can then develop an array of pricing strategies. Those strategies can outline both the high and low ends of your pricing spectrum, giving you parameters at each end.

The Importance of Execution

As you progress, you will clearly see areas that need improvement. While the gathering of information is important, you'll learn so much more in the execution. As you actually begin to optimize your business, you'll see the power of the information you've gained.

This is not just an intellectual process. The exercises are essential because they apply the intellectual information to your business. It's an entire process of execution, implementation, and results measurement. You then see the results of all that work in your business's success.

At the end of the day, it's all about the results. If you don't experience solid results, the information doesn't matter. Take the time to apply what you've learned and see its power as you execute it.

INTERNET MULTI-MILLIONAIRE STEPHEN PIERCE SHARES HIS ONLINE SUCCESS STRATEGIES WITH YOU FOR FREE ...

Introducing "Make Real Money on the Internet"!

This book will walk you through – step by step – what you need to do to start your online business. It doesn't matter if you are completely new to online marketing … if you've been online for a while but haven't been able to cash in yet … or if you've been online and are making decent money but not hitting the massive paydays you hear other people talking about … **Stephen will show you exactly what to do to hit the online jackpot**.

You will discover:

♦ How to get started on the Internet with minimum investment and minimum risk!
♦ How to work your own hours and get started WHILE you prepare to exit your full time job!
♦ How Stephen got started on the Internet without his own website or email list and at a time when he couldn't even afford a domain name or website hosting!
♦ How Stephen accidentally discovered that people would pay him for information on the Internet and how he transformed that into a half a million dollar business almost overnight!
♦ And much, much more!

To learn more or to reserve your **FREE** copy of this amazing book that promises to jumpstart your Internet career, please visit **www.MakeRealMoneyOnTheInternet.com** today!

BUSINESS OPTIMIZATION STRATEGY SERIES

Notes: